PET SOS
Fluffy the Cat

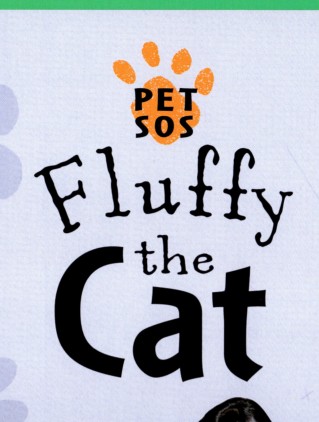

PET SOS

Fluffy the Cat

Tamsin Osler

Photography by Chris Fairclough

W

FRANKLIN WATTS

LONDON • SYDNEY

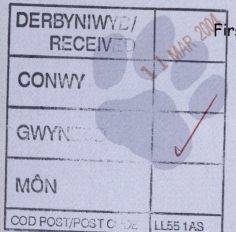
This edition 2004

First published in Great Britain by
Franklin Watts
96 Leonard Street
London EC2A 4XD

Franklin Watts Australia
45–51 Huntley Street
Alexandria NSW 2015

© 2001 Franklin Watts

ISBN: 0 7496 5599 2
Dewey Decimal Classification 636.8
A CIP catalogue record for this book is available from the British Library

Printed in Malaysia

Planning and production by Discovery Books
Editors: Tamsin Osler, Kate Banham
Design: Ian Winton
Art Direction: Jason Anscomb
Photography: Chris Fairclough

Acknowledgements
The publishers would like to thank Mr and Mrs Tanaka, their children George
and Ellie, the staff at the Chalfont St Peter Blue Cross Adoption Centre
and the Blue Cross for their help in the production of this book.

THE BLUE CROSS
ANIMAL WELFARE CHARITY

CONTENTS

The Blue Cross

This is Fluffy. She and her brother Browny came to live at the Blue Cross Adoption Centre at Chalfont St Peter when they were abandoned by their owners.

The Blue Cross is one of the oldest **animal charities** in Britain. First set up in 1897, it now runs eleven adoption centres, four hospitals and two centres for horses and ponies across the country.

Many animals come here because their owners don't want them any more. Some are here because they are too difficult for their owners to handle. Others come because they are sick or injured. The Blue Cross looks after them until new homes can be found for them.

The notice board has details of all the pets at the centre.

THE BLUE CROSS

– OPENING HOURS –

MONDAY TO FRIDAY 10.00am to 3.00pm
SATURDAY/SUNDAY & BANK HOLIDAYS
10.00am - 2.00pm
CLOSED CHRISTMAS DAY/BOXING DAY
AND NEW YEARS DAY
TEL: 01753 - 882560

Rabbits, guinea pigs and goats
live at the Chalfont
St Peter centre,
as well as cats.

The cattery

The cats and kittens who come to the centre live in an area called the **cattery**. They are kept in **runs**. Each cat has its own sleeping, feeding and play area, and its own **litter tray**.

The staff at the cattery know a lot about cats and kittens. One of their jobs is feeding the cats. They also clean out the runs and make sure the trays have fresh cat litter in them.

Every year about 8,000 animals are rescued by the Blue Cross. In 1999, they cared for 4,700 cats, and found new homes for 4,300 of them.

When cats first arrive at the centre, they are given a blood test to check that they are healthy. They are also **vaccinated** against some **infectious** diseases.

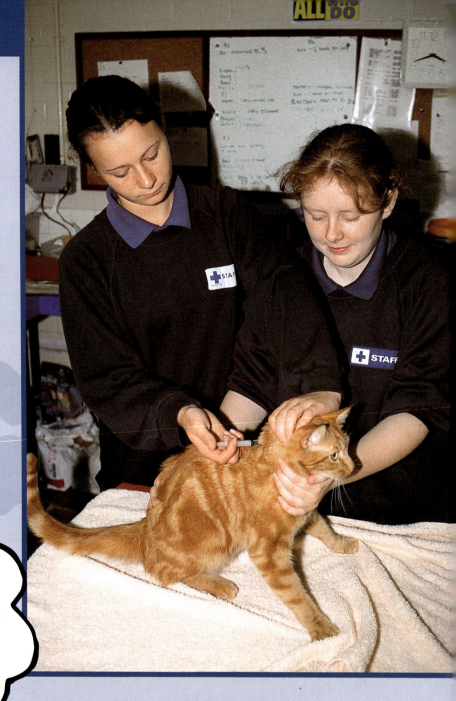

Once a cat is **rehomed**, the new owners have to make sure the vaccinations are kept up to date.

A kitten is normally first vaccinated when it is nine weeks old, and again when it is twelve weeks old. It should then have booster or top-up injections every year.

Some of the cats who are brought here have been knocked down by a car. Other cats, especially **strays**, are very thin and ill when they first arrive. The staff call the vet whenever a sick or injured animal is brought in.

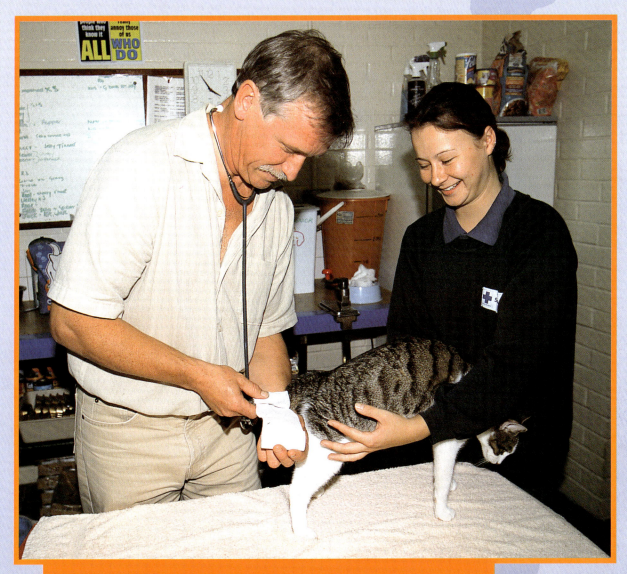

This cat's tail had been injured in an accident.

Meet the Tanaka family

The Tanaka family came to live in Britain in 1986. Before, when they lived in Japan, Mrs Tanaka often took in stray cats. Now she would like to have cats again. She wants her children, George and Ellie, to learn about caring for animals, too. The family have come to visit the Chalfont St Peter Blue Cross Adoption Centre.

A member of staff shows the Tanaka family some photos of the pets at the centre.

The centre's receptionist fills in a questionnaire.

The receptionist at the centre asks the Tanakas some questions about their home:
• Do they have a garden?
• Is their house near a busy road?
• Have they had cats or kittens before?
The answers help the Blue Cross to decide what kind of cat will be best for the family.

Choosing the cats

At the cattery the Tanakas see all sorts of different cats. There are long-haired cats and short-haired cats, in many different colours. There are older cats and there are kittens. George and Ellie fall in love with two cats called Fluffy and Browny.

George and Ellie meet Fluffy.

A few days later, one of the Blue Cross staff visits the Tanakas at their home to see if it is suitable for the cats. She looks around the house and the garden.

The Tanakas' garden will be a perfect place for the cats to play.

She decides that the Tanakas would be good owners, and tells them that they can adopt the two cats as soon as they like.

Did you know that nearly all ginger cats are male, and nearly all **tortoiseshell** cats are female?

Before the cats go to their new home, the Blue Cross makes sure their vaccinations are up to date.

The Blue Cross recommends that people have their cats tagged. A small electronic **microchip**, or tag, is placed under the skin at the back of the cat's neck. If the cat gets lost, the microchip can be **scanned** to find out the name and address of its owners.

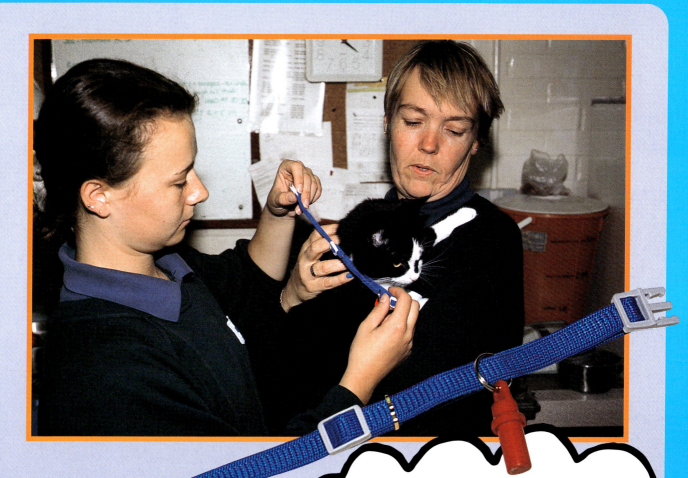

Collars can easily get caught on things, so it is not a good idea to put them on young kittens. Another reason is that kittens' necks are still growing, and the collar may become too tight.

Adult cats can also wear a collar with an **identity disc**, or tube. The collar should have a safety snap on it, so that the cat can slip out of it if it gets caught on anything.

Bringing the cats home

A few days later the family
go back to the centre
to fetch the cats.

Before a cat is rehomed, the new
owner has to sign an adoption form.
Among other things, the new owner has to
agree to look after the animal at all times,
to contact the Blue Cross if their pet goes
missing and to see that it is **neutered**,
if this hasn't already been done.

They fill in an
adoption form,
and one of the
staff puts the cats
into the carrier that
the Tanakas have
brought with them.

**The cats are
brought home in
a cat basket.**

The Tanakas have bought a plastic bed for the cats. They have lined it with a fleece to make it warm and comfortable for Fluffy and Browny. All cats spend a lot of time sleeping.

Cats are **solitary** animals. Although kittens like to play with one another, as they grow older cats spend more and more time on their own.

Looking after the cats

It is George's job to feed the cats. Often Ellie helps him. Fluffy and Browny are fed twice a day. They each have a fresh packet of cat food, but they also like dry food and crunchy biscuits.

It is important to make sure the cats have plenty of water to drink, too.

Each of the cats has its own feeding bowl.

It is best to feed animals at the same time each day. George and Ellie feed their cats before they go off to school in the morning. Then they feed them again when they come home from school in the afternoon.

George helps his mum to give the cats their flea treatment. This is a liquid that is squeezed on to the back of the cat's neck. It can also be a spray or a pill.

Cats also need to be **wormed**. You can buy worming treatment from the vet or a pet shop. This can be a pill, a liquid or **granules** that are mixed in the cat's food.

Cats and kittens can get worms and fleas. These are **parasites** that feed off the cats. If the cats are not treated for these, they will become weak and ill.

George's mum checks the cats' ears for **ear mites**. These are very tiny insects that live in the wax in a cat's ear. Ear mites can be painful, so it is important to check the cats' ears often.

Cats like to keep clean, and spend a lot of time washing themselves.

Cats sharpen their claws by scratching on rough surfaces. They use their claws for hunting, and for climbing too. A scratching post helps to keep their claws short and sharp.

Litter trays should only be filled with cat litter. They should be cleaned out regularly, otherwise cats won't use them.

One of George's jobs is to **groom** the cats with a special brush. Short-haired cats don't need grooming as often as long-haired cats. These need regular brushing to stop their fur becoming matted or tangled. It can also help to remove fleas.

Most cats love to have their coats groomed.

Hunting and playing

All cats are natural hunters. They learn hunting skills through play. George has bought each cat a small ball to chase, and a toy mouse made of special string. Both George and Ellie enjoy playing with the cats.

Fluffy and Browny are happy and healthy in their new home. They have become much-loved members of the family.

George and Ellie love their cats.

As well as caring for unwanted and abandoned animals, the Blue Cross helps people become good pet owners. Anyone can contact them for help and advice.

Glossary

Animal charity	An organization set up to look after animals in need.
Cattery	A place, or area, where cats are kept.
Ear mites	Very tiny insects that live in some animals' ears.
Granules	Small grains.
Groom	To brush an animal's coat to remove dirt and loose hairs.
Identity disc	A tag on a cat's collar that shows where it lives.
Infectious	An infectious disease is one that is easily passed on to other animals.
Litter tray	A cat's toilet tray to use indoors.
Microchip	A tiny electronic device.
Neutering	A simple operation that stops animals producing young.
Parasites	Insects and animals that feed off another animal.
Questionnaire	A form with questions to be filled in.
Rehome	To find a new home for a person or animal.
Run	A safe enclosed area for pets.
Scanned	Read with an electronic device.
Solitary	A solitary animal is one that prefers to be alone.
Stray	An animal that wanders from its home and gets lost.
Tortoiseshell	A pattern of black, brown, white and orange patches on a cat's coat.
Vaccinate	To give medicine or treatment that protects against diseases.
To worm	To remove worms from an animal's stomach.

Further information

The Blue Cross runs eleven adoption centres across the UK which you can visit. To find out the addresses and opening hours of the centres local to you, contact them on these telephone numbers:

Bromsgrove Adoption Centre
0121 453 3130

Burford Adoption Centre
01993 822483

Cambridge Adoption Centre
01223 350153

Chalfont St Peter Adoption Centre
01753 882560

Felixstowe Adoption Centre
01394 283254

Hertfordshire Adoption Centre
01438 832232

Northiam Equine & Adoption Centre
01797 252243

Southampton Adoption Centre
023 8069 2894

Thirsk Adoption Centre
01845 577759

Tiverton Adoption Centre
01884 855291

Torbay Adoption Centre
01803 327728

Other organizations that run rescue and adoption centres for cats and kittens include Cats' Protection and the Royal Society for the Prevention of Cruelty to Animals (RSPCA). You can contact them at:

Cats' Protection
17 Kings Road, Horsham
West Sussex RH13 5PN
Tel: 08702 099 099 www.cats.org.uk

RSPCA Enquiries Service
Wilberforce Way, Southwater
West Sussex RH13 9RS
Tel: 0870 333 5999 www.rspca.org.uk

In Australia you can contact:

Australian Cat Federation Inc
PO Box 2151
Rosebud Plaza, VIC 3939
Tel: (03) 5986 1119 www.acf.asn.au

Australian Animal Protection Society
10 Homeleigh Road
Keysborough, VIC 3173
Email: enquiries@aaps.org.au

RSPCA Australia
PO Box 265
Deakin West, ACT 2600
Tel: (02) 6282 8300 www.rspca.org.au

Index